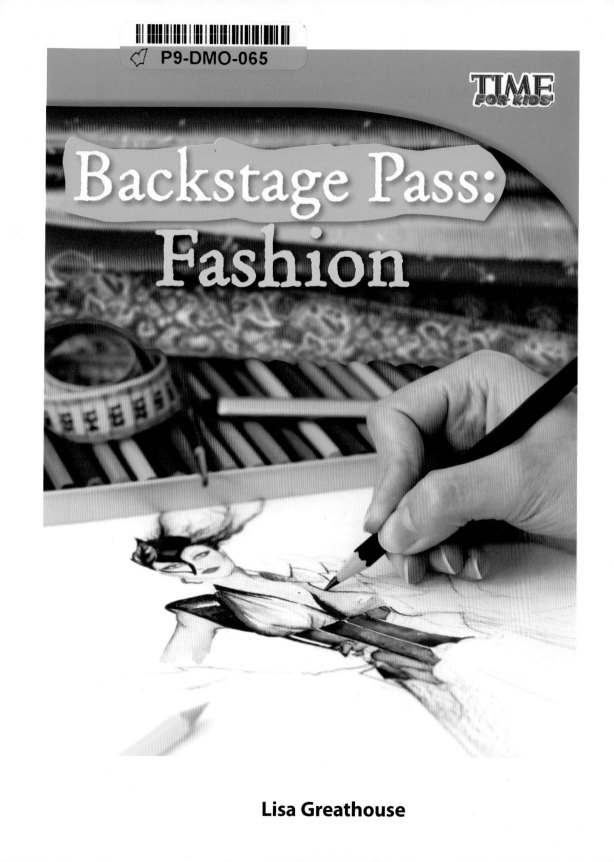

Backstage Pass: Fashion

P9-DMO-065

TIME FOR KIDS

Lisa Greathouse

Consultant

Timothy Rasinski, Ph.D.
Kent State University

Mary Katherine Rasinski,
Fashion Designer,
New York City

Publishing Credits

Dona Herweck Rice, *Editor-in-Chief*

Robin Erickson, *Production Director*

Lee Aucoin, *Creative Director*

Conni Medina, M.A.Ed., *Editorial Director*

Jamey Acosta, *Editor*

Heidi Kellenberger, *Editor*

Lexa Hoang, *Designer*

Stephanie Reid, *Photo Editor*

Rachelle Cracchiolo, M.S.Ed., *Publisher*

Image Credits

Cover: illustrat/Shutterstock; liewluck/shutterstock; p.3 Patrick Heagney 2009/iStockphoto; p.4 top to bottom: Rob Wilson/Shutterstock; AISPIX/Shutterstock; p.5 top to bottom: paphia/iStockphoto; grzhmelek/Shutterstock; Benis Arapovic/Shutterstock; p.6 top to bottom: Juanmonino/iStockphoto; karrapa/iStockphoto; p.7 top to bottom: The Granger Collection; Brand X/Getty Images; The Granger Collection; geotrac/iStockphoto; Jason_V/iStockphoto; Emmanuel Faure/Getty Images; p.8 top to bottom: talymel/iStockphoto; karrapa/iStockphoto; p.9 Slaven/Shutterstock; p.10-11 GreenPimp/iStockphoto; p.10 101images/Shutterstock; p.11 Andrey Armyagov/Shutterstock; donatas1205/Shutterstock; p.12-13 zhu difeng/Shutterstock; p.12 Sofy/Shutterstock; p.13 left to right: GoodMood Photo/Shutterstock; Elena Schweitzer/Shutterstock; p.14 Ugorenkov Aleksandr/Shutterstock; donatas1205/Shutterstock; p.15 top to bottom: Duncan P Walker/iStockphoto; Diego Cervo/Shutterstock; p.16 Kiselev Andrey Valerevich/Shutterstock; p.17 top to bottom: AVAVA/Shutterstock; CandyBox Images/Shutterstock; wwing/iStockphoto; John T Takai/Shutterstock; p.18 tirc83/iStockphoto; p.19 top to bottom: CandyBox Images/Shutterstock; paul prescott/Shutterstock; p.20 Frank Puterbaugh Bachman/Google; p.21 top to bottom: Ruslan Grechka/Shutterstock; esolla/iStockphoto; buriy/Shutterstock; p.22 Elena Elisseeva/Shutterstock; inset: crystalfoto/Shutterstock; p.23 kRie/Shutterstock; vesna cvorovic/Shutterstock; inset: crystalfoto/Shutterstock; p.24 AISPIX/Shutterstock; p.25 top: Sergey150770/Shutterstock; Garsya/Shutterstock; Dudaeva/Shutterstock; middle to bottom: Lorelyn Medina/Shutterstock; p.26-27 K2 images/Shutterstock; p.27 AFP/Getty Images/Newscom; p.28 left top to bottom: Elena Schweitzer/Shutterstock; Dudaeva/Shutterstock; Anthony Bolan/Shutterstock; middle: Karkas/Shutterstock; right: Karkas/Shutterstock; tan4ikk/Shutterstock; back: Dmitriev Lidiya/Shutterstock; p.29 left to right: AISPIX/Shutterstock; Picturenet/Photolibrary; p.32 Africa Studio/Shutterstock; background: Dmitriev/Shutterstock; paphia/shutterstock; severija/shutterstock; KLUISH VIKTORIA/Shutterstock; Mazzur/Shutterstock; severija/Shutterstock; back cover: buriy/Shutterstock.

Based on writing from *TIME For Kids*.

TIME For Kids and the *TIME For Kids* logo are registered trademarks of TIME Inc.
Used under license.

Teacher Created Materials

5301 Oceanus Drive
Huntington Beach, CA 92649-1030
http://www.tcmpub.com

ISBN 978-1-4333-3661-4

© 2012 Teacher Created Materials, Inc.
Printed in Malaysia
Thumbprints.27318

Table of Contents

Get the Look

Clothes show the world who we are. You might not think much about fashion when you get dressed in the morning. But everything you wear started with a fashion designer.

Grab your backstage pass. It's time to hit the **runway**. Let's find out what happens before a new dress lands in the window of your favorite store.

Head to Toe

Some fashion designers create clothes. Some specialize in shoes. Others may create purses or jewelry. Some designers do it all!

◀ Models show off a designer's new designs. ▼

A Creative Touch

Fashion designers are creative people. They need to have a **keen** eye for what looks good on people. They study fashion **trends**. That helps them figure out what kinds of clothes people will want to buy. They design everything from T-shirts to dresses and jeans to suits.

Designers look for ideas everywhere. They can be inspired by fashion from the past. Some designers are inspired by nature. The possibilities are endless.

The Long and Short of It

Hemlines, or the length of women's dresses and skirts, are just one of the ways in which women's fashion has changed over the years. In the 1970s, all three of these hemlines were popular:

- the daring mini (hemline at the thigh)
- the midi (hemline at the calf)
- the maxi (hemline at the ankle)

Today all three have come back in to style!

Fashion Milestones

Women's fashion has changed dramatically over time. Every decade has had its own look.

Year	Milestone
1800s	Forward thinking women begin to wear pants known as *bloomers*.
1900s	Big hats were decorated with feathers, ribbons, and flowers.
1940s	Women wear full skirts. New fabrics make it easier to wash and wear clothing.
1960s	Hemlines rise. The mini-skirt is popular. Fun new fabric patterns are designed.
1980s	This decade is marked by leg warmers, shoulder pads, and parachute pants.
Today	It seems that anything goes! Everyone brings his or her own personal style to fashion.

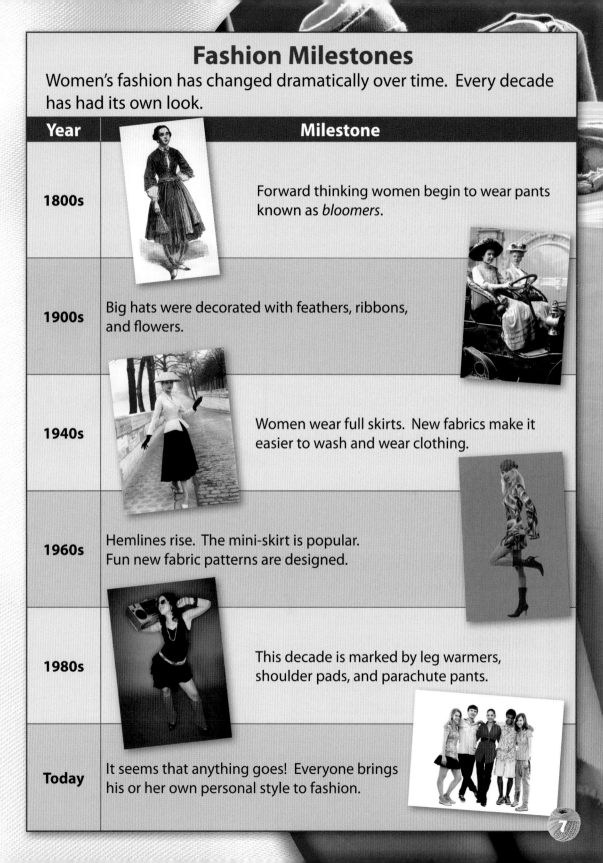

Imagine that a fashion designer has an idea for a dress. The designer thinks the style and colors will be popular next spring. The first step is to make a **sketch** of how the dress should look. The designer draws it on paper or on a computer.

A designer needs to be a skilled artist. But when designers pick up a pencil to sketch, they also need to think about something else—math!

The Artist's Eye

Designers think a lot about **proportion**. They use fabric to draw attention to certain areas of the body. They design clothes to create angles that **flatter** the body.

The lines, angles, and curves of this sketch come together to create a unique design. You are wearing math! ➤

So Many Choices!

Every **garment**, or piece of clothing, is designed with shapes, lines, and angles. This means the designer is using **geometry**. Will the bottom of a blouse have a straight edge, or will it be curved? Will the pants have straight legs or be **flared**? Should the T-shirt have a rounded collar or a V-neck? Should the V-neck have a wide angle? A fashion designer makes a lot of decisions.

These dresses have similar colors but very different styles.

These tops feature different necklines.

Geometry in Jeans

Jeans can have wide legs, skinny legs, or something in between. They can have pockets in every shape and size!

relaxed cut   straight cut   flare cut

bell bottom   slim cut   wide leg   regular cut

Now the designer must choose what kind of fabric to use. Choices include silk and lace, which are very expensive. Cotton is used in a lot of clothing. **Rayon**, **linen**, and **wool** are other choices. These fabrics all have their own **textures.**

Colors play a big role, too. A designer may choose colors based on the season in which the clothing will be in the stores. Lighter colors are often used in summer. You will see more pastels in the spring. Dark colors are more common in cooler weather.

Imagine all of the colorful creations designers will make with these fabrics.

Prints and Patterns

Many designers like working with prints or **patterns** on their fabrics. Some designers like making clothes with stripes. Some like polka dots. Some like lines that zigzag. Plaid is a pattern made of **intersecting** lines and colors.

Taking Measurements

The designer has chosen fabric and decided how the garment should look. Now the designer needs to make another drawing. This will be much more detailed than the sketch. This is a **technical drawing**.

A technical drawing shows all the measurements needed to make a sample version of the garment. That means the designer must figure out the length and width of every piece of the design. How long should the garment be? Should it be tight or loose? There can be dozens of measurements for one garment.

▲ measurement tools

Big Clothes for Small People

Designers have only been designing children's clothes for about 100 years. Before then, children wore adult clothing made in smaller sizes.

A designer reviews her sketches.

To make sure the dress fits the right way, the designer uses a **measuring tape**. A measuring tape is like a flexible ruler. The designer needs to make **accurate** measurements. This is also how he or she will know how much fabric to buy.

Now it is time for a sewing pattern to be made. A pattern can be made out of paper, cardboard, or tracing paper. It shows the real size of each part of the garment.

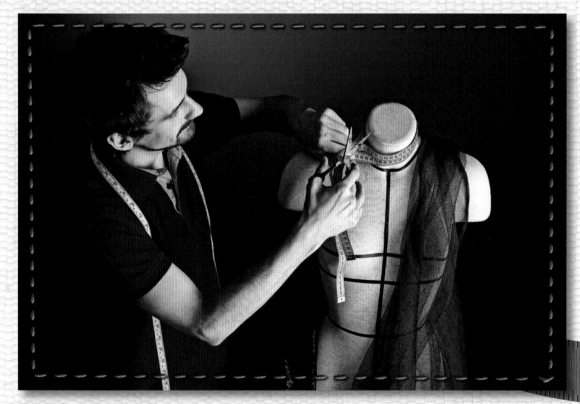

▲ A designer checks his measurements.

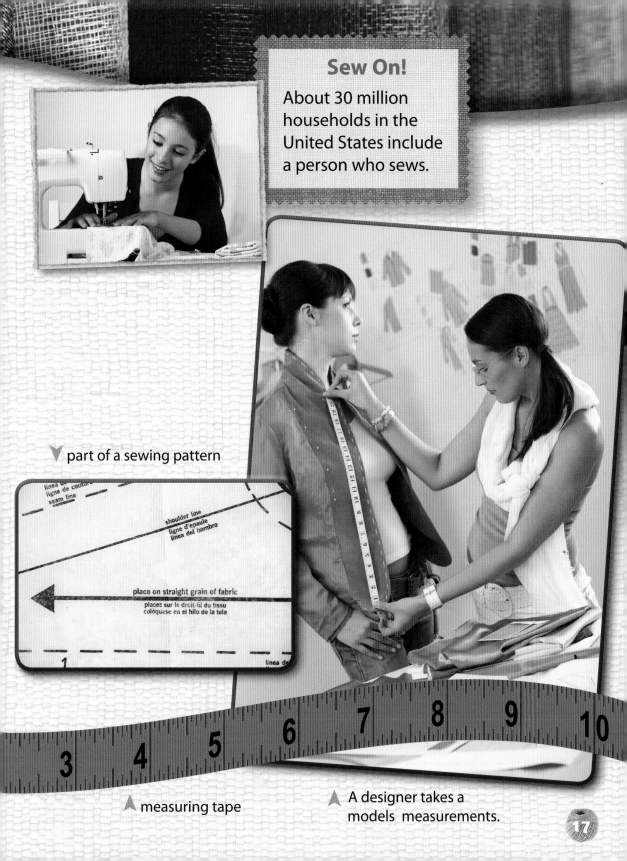

Sew On!

About 30 million households in the United States include a person who sews.

part of a sewing pattern

seam line
ligne de couture
linea de...

shoulder line
ligne d'epaule
linea del hombro

place on straight grain of fabric
placez sur le droit-fil du tissu
colóquese en el hilo de la tela

1

linea de...

3 4 5 6 7 8 9 10

measuring tape

A designer takes a models measurements.

Putting the Puzzle Together

A sewing pattern looks like a bunch of cut-out shapes. When the shapes are put together, they form the whole garment. It's almost like putting together a puzzle.

The pattern shapes are pinned onto the fabric. Then the fabric is cut in the shape of each piece. This is when measurements are really important! You can waste a lot of fabric if you don't cut the pattern just right.

A designer must plan each piece of clothing carefully. ➤

The Big Boss

Designers can work for themselves and sell their designs to companies. Or they can work for a company that will own their designs. Some designers set up their own companies.

Finally, the sewing begins! The designer creates a sample. All the cut-out pieces of fabric are pinned together. The dress is fitted on a model or on a **form**. Buttons and zippers may need to be added. Most of the sewing is done on sewing machines. But some dresses have beads or sequins. These need to be added by hand.

The dress will probably need to be **tailored** so it looks just right. The sleeves might need to be longer. The waist may need to be taken in. The length may need to be shortened. That means more measuring!

History of the Sewing Machine

People have been sewing by hand for over 20,000 years. The first American **patent** for a sewing machine was issued to Elias Howe in 1846. This made producing clothing faster and cheaper.

dress form

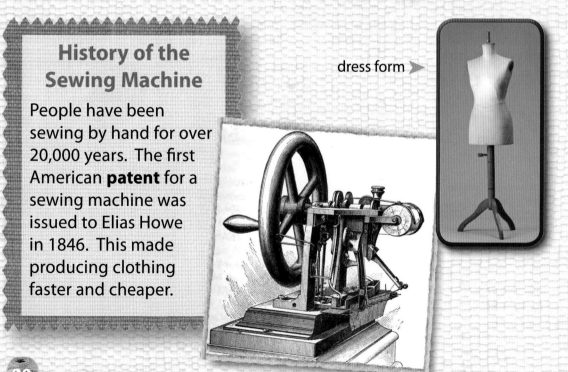

Ways of Sewing

The sewing machine allows designers to produce larger amounts of clothing faster. Hand sewing lets designers add special details to their work. Each stitch is sewn just right, and a lot of hard work and attention goes into every bead or button.

The Business of Fashion

When the sample is perfect, it becomes the **prototype**. This is what all the other dresses will look like. Patterns are created to make the dress in different sizes.

Once the dress is made, it's ready to sell in stores. Now comes the business side of fashion design. The designer uses math to know what price to charge for the dress.

Store Buyers

Designers show their garments to store buyers. These are the people who decide what clothing to sell in stores. Math helps buyers figure out how much to buy.

$85

First, the designer must add up all the costs to see how much money was spent making one dress. This includes things like fabric, buttons, zippers—even thread. There may be other costs, too. The designer will need to pay people to sew the dresses. There are shipping costs if the dresses are **manufactured** far away. These costs are added together. Then the total cost is divided by the number of dresses being made.

Hidden Costs

Designers who work for themselves may need to include other costs. Items like sewing equipment, and office space are part of a designer's expenses.

Expenses		Amount	Price
Fabric		15 yards	$100.00
Buttons		10 pieces	$2.50
Zippers		1 set	$0.75
Ribbon		15 yards	$15.00
Trim		5 yards	$15.00
Seamstress/labor		40 hours	$600.00
Shipping		to Paris, France	$85.00
TOTAL			**$818.25**

Now the designer has to decide how much to charge stores for the dress. The designer should charge more than it cost to make the dress. The difference between the cost and the price the buyer pays for it is **profit**. Designers must make a profit to keep their businesses running. This money is used to buy fabric and other supplies needed for the next project.

Star Power

Making clothes can be very expensive. That means it can sometimes be difficult for designers to make a profit. Sometimes designers ask celebrities to put their names on new designs so that clothes will sell. These clothes are some of the most popular today.

Global Glamour

London, Milan, Paris, and New York are leaders in the fashion industry. Every year each city hosts Fashion Week. All the major designers present their latest creations on the runway. People watch the styles and trends in these cities closely.

Making a Profit

$50.00	$100.00	$200.00

The designer buys supplies for $50.00.

The designer sells the dress to the store buyer for $100.00. The designer makes a profit of $50.00.

The customer buys the dress from the store for $200.00. The store makes a profit of $100.00.

Now it is the store's turn to make a profit. That means the price of the dress must be raised. Finally, the price tag goes on the dresses. The fashion designer and the store both hope customers will buy them!

Being a fashion designer is an exciting and creative job. It also requires a solid understanding of math. Designers must be able to use geometry. They must be able to take careful measurements. A designer must also be a businessperson. Math skills help make the business profitable.

In fashion a designer wears many different hats—maybe even designs some of them!

Glossary

accurate—free of mistakes or errors

flared—spreading outward

flatter—to make attractive

form—a shape used to help fit clothing

garment—a piece of clothing

geometry—an area of mathematics concerned with the study of shapes and objects

intersecting—meeting or crossing at one or more points

keen—mentally sharp and clever

linen—a smooth, strong cloth made from flax

manufactured—produced

measuring tape—a tool used by designers to get accurate measurements of a garment

patent—an official right to make, use, or sell an invention or design

patterns—arrangements of shapes, lines, letters, numbers, or colors that are repeated; guides or models

profit—the money made that is more than the total expenses

proportion—a balanced or pleasing arrangement

prototype—a test piece

rayon—a fabric made from fibers that have been produced chemically

runway—a narrow platform people walk on to model clothing at a fashion show

sketch—a rough and quickly drawn picture

tailored—altered or repaired clothing

technical drawing—a detailed drawing that shows the exact measurements of a garment

textures—the feel or look of different surfaces

trends—the latest styles

wool—a fabric made out of the thick undercoat of animals, such as sheep

Index

About the Author

Lisa Greathouse grew up in Brooklyn, N.Y., and graduated from the State University of New York at Albany with a bachelor's degree in English and journalism. She was a reporter, a writer, and an editor for The Associated Press for 10 years, covering news on everything from science and technology to business and politics. She has also been a magazine editor and a writer for education publications and a university website. Today, she works as a writer at the Disneyland Resort, where she oversees an employee magazine. In her spare time, she enjoys visiting Mickey Mouse and riding Space Mountain. She is married with two children and resides in Southern California.